# Swim Naked, Defy Gravity &

### 99 OTHER ESSENTIAL THINGS
### TO ACCOMPLISH
### BEFORE TURNING 30

# Colleen Rush

BlueHen Books
New York

BLUEHEN BOOKS
Published by The Berkley Publishing Group
A division of Penguin Group (USA) Inc.
375 Hudson Street
New York, New York 10014

Copyright © 2004 by Penguin Group (USA) Inc.
Book design by Tiffany Estreicher
Cover design by Charles Björklund

PRINTING HISTORY
BlueHen trade paperback edition / September 2004

Library of Congress Cataloging-in-Publication Data

Rush, Colleen.
   Swim naked, defy gravity & 99 other essential things to accomplish before
turning 30 : a checklist / Colleen Rush—1st ed.
      p. cm.
   ISBN: 0-425-20093-0
   1. Young adults—Life skills guides.   I. Title: Swim naked, defy gravity and 99
other essential things to accomplish before turning 30.   II. Title.

HQ799.5 R87 2004
646.7'0084'2—dc22                                              2004048506

Printed in the United States of America

10   9   8   7   6   5   4   3   2   1

*To Kelley, Lynnet, and Meredith,*
*my silly, strong, and devoted*
*sisters who taught me the*
*important stuff.*

# Swim Naked, Defy Gravity &

**99** OTHER ESSENTIAL THINGS
TO ACCOMPLISH
BEFORE TURNING 30

Swim naked.

Never underestimate the primal power of nudity and water. Maybe we have some kind of instinctive attraction to water, like it's a metaphorical reconnection to the floating, safe feeling of being in the womb. Maybe it's because after a certain age, shopping for or wearing a bathing suit can feel like a kickboxing session on your self-esteem. Whatever. Bobbing, diving, and doing naked somersaults are a blast, and it's even better when you're not alone. Skinny-dipping is one of those forever-bonding experiences that you'll always carry around in the back of your head. The smallest things can trigger a flashback, whether it's the sight of a pond, the memory of a person, or just some dull day when you think your life is so boring and you remember the naughty, giddy feeling of being naked out in the open. The funny thing is, you'll never recall the self-conscious "They'll see my dimpled butt and droopy boobs" moments of doubt. Or, if you do, it's closely followed by the realization that if you had let your neurotic side win, you would've missed out big-time. So anytime you have to choose between exposing yourself, flaws and all, or sitting safely on the sidelines to watch—at work, in love, and throughout your life—well, maybe it won't be such a difficult decision.

# Break all
# of your parents'
# arbitrary rules.

It goes without saying that curfews and groundings are a thing of the past, but one of the greatest things about growing up is having your own little haven where you can do what you damn well please. It's an awesome opportunity to flaunt all of those nitpicky, random, authoritarian rules your parents invented to torture you. Leave the refrigerator door wide open while you decide what you're in the mood to eat. Open two, no, *three* boxes of cereal at once, even if you still have a few tablespoons left in another. Skate through your house in socks until they're threadbare. Only make your bed when guests come over. Leave the cap off the toothpaste. Burn incense. Turn on every light in the house and go away for the weekend. Parents have every right to lay down the law when you're living under their roof, and no doubt some of those household policies kept them from strapping you to it. But getting to that stage in your life where you can defy those orders not only means you've reached the point of true independence, you also get to start making up your own ridiculous house rules, like "No sappy Meg Ryan movies allowed in the DVD player" or "Refrigerator must hold dark chocolate at all times."

Grow
something.

B uy seeds and plant anything that'll come to life under your care, whether it's a Chia Pet, herbs in a box, or something more ambitious, like a ficus tree. Nurturing is in our nature, but sometimes we need more solid proof of our skills before we take on bigger roles, like pet owner, girlfriend, wife, or mother. Watching a tiny brown speck turn into a rooting, blooming, breathing thing is a thrill in itself, but taking responsibility for its livelihood is a small-scale lesson in selflessness and sacrifice. From the moment the first green shoots peek out of the soil, your plant is a daily, living reminder that you can nourish and provide. Besides, if it never sprouts or if it turns brown and dies, there will always be more seeds to practice on until you get it right.

Dump toxic friends.

**She's** the girl you've known since preschool, or the college roommate who won't lose your number, or the former coworker who still insists on monthly get-togethers. She's a lead weight on your life, calling only when she has a favor to ask or a crisis for you to solve, and she's the constant dark cloud in your world—always raining on your parade and showering her bad vibes all over when you really need support. You still return her calls, offer your friendship, and let her bring you down, because your good-girl guilt won't let you cut the cord. We outgrow friendships all the time, but instead of whittling down the inner circle to the best of the bunch, we hold on to old friendships that are past their due, because a confrontation is even less appealing than sitting through another dreadful encounter with this punk friend. But baggage is baggage—carrying her around is a major drain on your emotional energy, and your real relationships suffer, too. Even the best of friends will eventually start dodging you when your pity pal is around. Toxic people are like those mysterious containers of leftovers in your refrigerator—you avoid tossing them because they might still be good, but they only get more pungent and dangerous with time.

# Speak a foreign language.

There's an old joke that goes like this: What do you call a person who only speaks one language? An American. But the joke's only funny for about a second, and then it's just sad . . . and true. I've visited countless countries where I didn't speak the language, but knowing even a few simple words, how to ask for directions, and say "I'm sorry" in the native tongue meant the difference between getting a hand and getting the finger. Learning another language is an awkward, humbling experience because you're wrong 98 percent of the time you open your mouth. But those rare moments when you are able to connect with someone in their own language, to ask, "Is the water supposed to be green?" or say, "These mojitos make my teeth numb. Thank you," are worth all of the humiliation.

# Buy a kick-ass mattress.

**I**f you've slept on saggy, hand-me-down mattresses for twenty-odd years, this one's a no-brainer. Splurging on the perfect mattress is like finding the perfect man. They're both just soft and firm and big enough, they comfort you through sickness and sadness, and you look forward to snuggling up with them at the end of a long day.

# Draw and frame a self-portrait.

$\mathcal{G}$**rab** a pen or brush and paint a picture of who you are. Stick-figure simple or cut-out collage or realistic sketch, putting your likeness on paper is the ultimate form of self-expression. Anyone can draw a picture based on appearance, but only you know yourself well enough to illustrate the whole you, inside and out. Give yourself time to go through drafts and revisions, like any great artist, and focus on features, themes, and passions that define not only the way you look, but the common threads that run through your life. The colors you love, the quirky objects you collect, what you daydream about, your everyday existence—all of those seemingly random bits of information, ideas, and things belong in a self-portrait. Think of it as a picture with secrets to tell. The point isn't to create a piece of art, but to capture how you see yourself at this point in your life.

# Stop chronic over-apologizing.

$\mathcal{S}$aying "sorry" is generally the polite thing to do when you've committed a faux pas or stepped on someone's toes, but reflexively apologizing for every little snafu, regardless of whether you're at fault, is a pathological problem for some of us. If you've ever caught yourself muttering "sorry" to the rude deli guy who screws up your order or to no one in particular over seriously trivial things, like when you trip, drop your keys, or the lead in your pencil breaks, you're part of the club. Far from a harmless habit, over-apologizing makes you seem spineless and mousy, as if your very existence is reason enough to repent. Giving off that wilting violet vibe may have worked one hundred years ago, but it's likely to get you steamrolled flat today. Be more vigilant with your words and what you apologize for. Backing over your neighbor's cat certainly qualifies for a "sorry," but brushing against someone in a crowded subway warrants an "excuse me" at most.

# Create your own sisterhood.

I'm one of those lucky girls who was born with soul sisters. The rowdy gang of couples my parents ran with had daughters my age, and we were a motley crew from the beginning. There are pictures of us beaming from swing sets in the park, striking a boob-stuffed pose in old-fashioned bathing suits on the steps of the family cabin, standing with pimply Homecoming dates—a library's worth of moments. We had plenty of fights and a few periods when we barely spoke, along with jealousy, fierce competition, hurt feelings, and all of the typical ups and downs that go with honest relationships. Through countless boyfriends, magnificent teenage dramas, divorces, babies, new jobs, cross-country moves and every tragedy or success a thirty-year-old girl can have in so many years, our kindred connection has weathered it all. We've cried together; gotten screaming, cackling drunk and held each other's hair out of the toilet bowl; laughed until our cheeks ached; covered each other's asses; sworn to break the legs and balls of any man who hurts one of us; and confessed secrets that will die with us. No woman should turn a certain age without having—by right of birth or over years of searching—a band of such wily, devoted girlfriends. Even when you find the love of your life or collect new pockets of friends, these are the women who fill a permanent spot in your soul. They know and adore the real you, not in spite of your history, but because of it.

# Travel solo.

Do a semester abroad. Take an exotic vacation. Hit the highway for a weekend road trip. The important thing is to do it all by yourself—at least once—to get in touch with the raw, unfiltered essence of you. Nothing hones your survival instincts or demonstrates what you're really made of like being surrounded by the unfamiliar, especially when you're alone and lost, hungry, and don't speak the language. We only ever hear about the dangers of being a woman alone in a strange land, but there's something to be said about stripping away the safety net. It sharpens your intuition and, in many ways, restores your sense of trust because you have to rely on the kindness of strangers to make the most of your adventure. Best of all, you can immerse yourself in the local culture without being weighed down by your own baggage. No one knows if you've recently gained ten pounds or gotten dumped by a boyfriend or been fired from a job—since no one knows *you*. When you're alone, you can take more risks and be more daring with no fear of it following you home.

# Develop a Plan B.

**I**f you win the lottery. If you get hit by a tractor. If you meet the right guy. There will always be "ifs" in your life that you shouldn't overthink. But when it comes to ifs about your livelihood and independence (If all else fails; If you finally snap at work after years of fruitless sucking up; If you get sick of doing what you went to school for), you should always think about your backup plan. Do you see yourself starting a business? Going back to school? Chucking it all and traveling for a year? There are two simple reasons you need to create your own escape plan. One, unless crashing in your old room under your parents' roof sounds appealing, your plan is the emergency exit door that'll keep your life moving in the right direction. Rather than getting tripped up by the obstacles and setbacks that come your way, having a vague idea of your other options can help you avoid the pre-midlife-crisis meltdown that usually comes with major, unexpected changes. Two, your Plan B points to what you really want—not what you're willing to settle for. When you're dreaming up a new angle for your life, chances are you're not thinking about another boring desk job or a steady paycheck. You're planning for your freedom, and your perfect-world scenario naturally includes ideas that hint at your true passions.

# Know your friends' family tree.

Where I grew up, "How's your mama?" is the sweetest greeting you can ask for, because it means you're in the presence of someone who actually cares what the answer is. To ask the question, you have to know about my mama, which means you've probably heard about my sisters, brother, aunts, uncles, cousins, and every other character I'm related to who's worth mentioning. There are people who flow in and out your life like the tide, but your friends have whole histories that you need to absorb in order to really know and love them. You should make the effort to learn the key relatives' names and how they fit into the family puzzle. You should ask about their feuds and get her to tell you the classic stories about the crazy ones and find out a few of their dark secrets. Then, when you sit down for coffee or catch her on a bad day, you can ask things like, "Has your nephew started walking?" or "Is your cousin out of the institution?"—questions that underscore your connection to her. Knowing basic background information about your friends keeps you plugged in to their worlds instead of totally engrossed in your own, and fosters a genuine bond that goes beyond a casual friendship. It's comforting to know someone actually listens and remembers those little details about who you are, because it underlines the fact that you're not alone. Besides, being privy to what goes on in their family can make yours seem really sane.

# Embrace your inner eight-year-old.

*S*omewhere underneath the dry-cleaned pants and polished, pointy shoes, and before the fruity diets and self-conscious dread kicked in, there's the girl we all were when life was still a bit mysterious and unthreatening. She still wants to tell corny jokes and giggle when someone farts. When things aren't going her way, she'd like to pout or throw a hissy fit. Given the chance, she'd paint her toenails ten different colors and deftly sculpt her mashed potatoes into works of art. If school (or work) is boring, she wouldn't think twice about faking sick to stay home. She doesn't need a reason to hold her best friend's hand or talk to trees, cats, and old people. Most of us tied her up when it was time to fit in, because it wasn't cool to be so brash and feisty. But she's still in there, under the serious façade and uptight manners, and it's okay to unleash her every now and then. Let her make a few decisions, like what to do on a Saturday or whether to eat dessert, and find her again when you're lost or heartbroken and need to channel her fierce little spirit.

# Read:

*Women's Bodies, Women's Wisdom*

by Christiane Northrup, M.D.

If you've ever been curious about the power of women's intuition, and care about your health and the well-being of every XX-chromosome carrier you know, this book can help you make the kind of mind-body connection that could save your life. Our bodies are fascinating and sometimes scary, but there's a weird disconnect between what we know is right and how we treat our bodies. We say we're goddesses and that the female body is a sacred temple, but we treat it like a halfway house. Taking responsibility for your health means more than getting prescriptions filled and handing over co-payments; it takes a commitment to improving your diet, reducing your stress, and changing other conditions that are closely linked to common medical problems. We're all guilty of ignoring the basic wisdom that we know and feel about our bodies, from smoking too much to marathon TV-watching to living with a toxic job environment, but sooner or later you have to accept your role in causing, preventing, or healing the aches and illnesses you suffer from.

# Build a raging
# campfire.

nyone can whiz a container of lighter fluid onto a pile of wood and light it on fire, but it takes a bit more know-how and finesse to stoke up the kind of blaze that'll burn until the last marshmallow is devoured. Aside from the obvious reasons it's a good survival skill to know; this Girl Scout wisdom empowers you with the *grrrrr*-factor. Good bonfires are sexy, but for whatever reason, building them always gets put under the column of men's work, as if they've got the biological privilege of playing with fire. When a girl can cobble together the wood, leaves, and kindling, and light up an inferno that cuts through the dark, it shatters the notion that we can't fend for ourselves. The ability to make fire screams "Capable!" and "Independent!" and "Badass!" So light it up, Earth Mama. The fire won't be the only thing roaring.

# Make the first move.

**D**on't wait for the perfect guy, the ultimate job, or the adventure of a lifetime to fall out of the sky and land in your lap. It doesn't work that way. Yet somewhere along the way, we get it in our heads that if we're nice and smart and think we deserve the best, our stellar karma makes the good things in life just effortlessly fall into place without having to pursue them. But you blow so many chances when you wait. Why not be a little more impatient? If you've ever been to a sample sale, where otherwise sane and demure women will growl and arm-wrestle you for a blouse, you understand how a moment's hesitation can screw you out of a sweet deal. The same concept applies to those things you really, *really* want but are too chicken to go for. You've got to get over your meekness and be willing to risk a wee bit of your dignity if you want it badly enough.

# Know the other mouth-to-mouth.

$\mathcal{T}$ake a CPR refresher class and brush up on those first aid skills you haven't thought about since high school gym class. It's hard to imagine the unthinkable happening—that someone you love or even a stranger passing by might suddenly need emergency resuscitation—and not panic at the thought of trying to save a life. You need confidence as much as competence when you're in an emergency situation, and reviewing what you know every now and then is the only way to feel comfortable doing it.

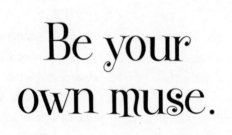

Be your
own muse.

$\mathcal{G}$reat artists and brilliant minds throughout history have given credit to the luminous ladies who inspired them. But why does being a muse have to involve giving your mojo away and channeling your energy into someone else's masterpiece? And why should you seek inspiration from outside your own realm? Whatever your artistic interests, you don't have to look to other people to stir your creative juices. You've got enough years behind you to have plenty of wisdom, insight, and energy to inspire your own work—it's just a matter of tapping into it. When you use your own experience and passion to create, whether you're redecorating your living room, writing a short story, or mixing music for your next all-nighter, it's real. Zone in on your own existence for ideas, from the snippets of conversation you hear every day and what you see on your way to work to the textures that thrill your skin and the bizarre-o dreams you have after eating Indian food. Focus on who you are and where you came from, and how that affects the ideas and tastes and colors that appeal to you. In short, inspire yourself. Being your own muse means you can take all the credit for being brilliant.

# Master a signature family recipe.

**I**t's an edible homage to your family. Adopting a food tradition is a sign that you've come full circle and can, after years of therapy or telling people you're an orphan, appreciate where you came from. You've started a few of your own customs, like ordering takeout on Sundays or using your oven for extra shoe storage space. You've done everything to prove that you're not simply a carrier of your family's whacked genes. Of course you love them and all of their quirks, but your post-college years are all about establishing an identity outside of your family role and snipping the ties that kept you tethered to the ongoing dramas. You're attracted to guys who couldn't be more opposite, and you stake out a life that your parents don't wholly approve of. Whenever you go home, you wear, do, and say things to reinforce your separateness, as if to say, "We're related, but I'm my own girl now." But for all that you do to create distance or otherness, eventually you realize that they're not so bad after all. When you can re-create those dishes that instantly take you home, you've made peace with your past.

# Quit
something.

Whoever said, "Quitters never win, and winners never quit" probably never worked for a soul-sucking tyrant, or signed up for a team sport or project from hell and immediately regretted it. But the rest of us have. And sticking it out for the sake of not being a quitter is flat-out demented. It's one thing to be determined and persistent and loyal, but if you've got a job that's slowly, painfully tearing you to pieces (hint: you cry on the way to and from work) or any other so-called commitment that's eating your time, patience, and self-confidence, throwing in the towel is the most liberating and quiet revenge you can have. But quitting isn't about swiping office supplies and mooning your boss on the way out the door or any other bridge-burning move that jeopardizes your class act. It's about putting your foot down and saying, "No"—that word we find so difficult to utter because we're afraid someone will get mad or not like us anymore. Walking away means you know you're worth more, and aren't afraid to fly without a safety net to find your niche.

# Find the perfect red lipstick.

Nothing gives you an instant face-lift like the right shade of red, but there are a zillion variations of the same hue, so finding the one that suits your skin tone can be hell—almost as frustrating as the search for the perfect mate who can ride out your mood swings. Make it your mission to scour drugstores, makeup counters, and your friends' beauty stashes to track down the ultimate color. (Murphy's Law: when you find the right shade, they'll discontinue it, so stock up.) A sweep of the right red over your lips won't do anything for world peace, but when you're looking and feeling like bedraggled roadkill, a punch of color can make you feel less so.

# Negotiate
# for something
# expensive.

It takes genuine moxie to stare someone in the face and say, "I won't pay a dime more." Granted, the mere thought of shelling out wads of cash, even for something you really need, can be nerve-racking, and most of us would probably ask a boyfriend, dad, or brother to step in to do the wheeling and dealing. But the "Leave it to Mister" mentality is *so* 1952. We should take our cue from the way men bargain. They never waver, even when they have no clue what they're doing (like driving aimlessly for hours rather than cracking open a map), and they have no qualms about pushing their luck to get extra perks. Their attitude is, "If they're gonna take my money, they'd better earn it." We generally cave at the slightest hint of confrontation, and think, "I'm giving them my money, so they'll play nice and be fair." So we walk away thinking, "I got shafted because I'm a girl," and it sours the whole experience. In truth, it takes a little bit of both philosophies to get the best deal. When you do your research and question everything over and over until you actually understand what you're paying for (and whether it's the right price), you'll know when you're getting a fair shake and when you're being taken for a ride. An infusion of confidence also gives you the gumption to ask for free delivery, installation, a new coat of paint, or other little upgrades to sweeten the deal. Once you hone your poker face in high-stakes buying, being a girl is actually your secret weapon in negotiations because they expect you to crumble.

Google
yourself.

There's an Olympic skeleton racer from Utah, a 4-H girl in Louisiana who raises grand-champion Brahman heifers for livestock shows, a woman who lived in Philadelphia in 1992 and was jilted by a guy who still wants to apologize, and several other women out there with my name on the Internet. I found stories I wrote ten years ago for my college newspaper, and two guys who really don't like the sex columns I've written—one a disgruntled columnist in Bombay, the other a Texas comedian who calls himself "Cowboy Bill." It's a trip to find yourself in unexpected places on the Internet, and even more so to get a peek into the lives of people who share your moniker. Even though you'll probably never meet face to face, you can't help but feel a little proud to be connected in some way. Seeing how we're all entwined out there in cyberspace makes you feel a little less anonymous and insulated.

Hold your booze.

You know the type. She's the life of the party for about twenty minutes, but has three too many drinks in her and quickly turns into a train wreck. You don't want to be That Girl, so if you can't have a few glasses of wine or a cocktail or two over the course of a night without turning into a screaming, sobbing, or slurring mess, it's time to rethink your drinking habits. Either cut back completely or slow down and switch between your drink of choice and something nonalcoholic. It's one thing when you're in or just out of college to get blackout drunk—it's not pretty or classy, but at least it's forgivable—but once you start filtering into more sophisticated affairs, like weddings or business dinners, doing body shots and dirty dancing by yourself is just tacky. There will be nights that you overdo it occasionally, but you don't want to be known as the wobbly, puke-prone drunk in your social network.

Track down
your best
friend from
kindergarten.

When you're six years old, it's practically impossible to be anything but yourself. You don't know how to be judgmental or cliquey at that age, so your best buddy was someone you jelled with for the real reasons: you could make each other laugh till milk spewed out of your nose and you both agreed that boys had cooties. Now that you're all grown up, reconnect with her even if you think you've got absolutely nothing in common. Of course you've changed, but how much? Chances are, the only thing different is the superficial stuff that didn't matter back then, like how much you weigh, what's in your bank account, and your love life (because you finally figured out that cooties aren't all bad). What's striking is how *little* you've changed since then. Finding that friend is a good reminder that you probably knew more about the important things in life in kindergarten.

# Masturbate.

Whether you admit to it or not is your decision. But every liberated, curious, healthy woman who wants a good sex life should spend some solo time exploring her own erotic avenues. Masturbating isn't dirty or shameful or a sign that you can't get any. In fact, knowing how to flip your own switch is actually a boon to any romantic relationship. When you've mastered the subtleties and techniques of masturbating, you can show him how it's done—and, unless he's an uptight freak, he'll truly appreciate it. Not knowing what turns you on and gets you *there* yet hopping into the sack with a guy and expecting him to be an expert on *your* orgasm, well, that's called the blind leading the blind in bed. It's a matter of physiological fact that we're built differently and are a bit more complicated to please, compared to most guys, who typically conquer the art of fiddling with themselves before they can walk or form complete sentences. But our orgasms take more time and finesse. You simply can't expect a guy to get it if you're still mystified, too. It's like asking a complete stranger to buy you a pair of shoes—if he doesn't know your size or style, you'll end up with duds.

Write a
complaint
letter.

To the department store that overcharged you or the health insurance company that jerks you around or the landlord who won't fix anything, put your gripes on paper instead of simmering over the injustice. When you're young and naïve, you think you have no alternatives but to suck it up and learn your lesson the hard way. But you've got to get to a point when you fight back if you're swindled or treated like dirt. Nasty looks, rude voice mails, and curse-laden confrontations will only get you so far, but writing a sharp, articulate letter outlining how you got a raw deal and how the company or person can make up for it gets results. The simple fact that you took the time to pen your complaint catches their attention, and is more likely to net an apology and action.

# Claim your granny panties.

You know, the giant, ugly, soft ones that give your butt a hug and make you feel dreamy when you're bloated? Don't deny you've got 'em. They really don't deserve the bad rep. When you're loafing on Sunday or PMS-ing or interviewing for your dream job, your granny panties are there for you 100 percent. Anyone can flash thong, but only a woman who is at ease in her own skin and truly liberated can proudly wear the unsexy skivvies. Eventually, you have to accept that things like comfort, confidence, and an unfettered butt crack are way more important to your self-esteem than foxy lingerie.

# Make brownies from scratch.

Too many things in life seem so much harder than they really are. Homemade brownies, for example. You'd think baking them required five hours and a degree in chemistry, but it's as simple as melting chocolate and stirring in eggs, sugar, flour, and oil. Whipping up a batch is as easy as those pour-stir-bake boxed mixes, but so much more gratifying. Because you know people are thinking, "She's smart, beautiful, *and* she makes her own brownies?!" when you say "I made 'em all by myself." But following a simple recipe for real brownies is just the tip of the iceberg. It's only a matter of time before you discover and conquer all of the other things you thought were impossible.

Exorcise the words "like" and "you know" from your vocabulary.

Have you ever listened to yourself talking, and realized that your powers of description are limited to those three words? "So I was like, 'No way,' and he was all, 'Yes way,' you know?" The valley girl ramble isn't a crime when you're gossiping and kvetching with a bunch of girlfriends, but it becomes such an ingrained part of your speech that it can infiltrate all of your other conversations, whether you're talking to your boss, a client, or a complete stranger. Although you don't need Shakespearean diction or an SAT vocabulary, certain teenybopper up-speak words are distracting and can stop a good conversation in its tracks. You get to a point when the words that tumble out of your mouth are more powerful and telling than your snappy shoes or flawless hair. Striking a few of those girlie expressions makes you sound more articulate and interesting . . . even if the E! channel is your primary news source.

# Find your religion.

For a long time, religion was simply church and nuns and Bible stories to me. I attended Catholic school and went through all of the motions that being Catholic required, but I never really felt spiritual or that I was part of something bigger. Somewhere between twenty-five and twenty-eight, when I got past the natural anxiety over how I would support myself and carve out a life of my own, I found my religion. It's not the traditional, organized kind, with church on Sunday and uncomfortable shoes and itchy, nude pantyhose. It's whatever gives me peace, hope, and a sense of connection with people around me. Like cooking dinner for my artist friends, who schlep to crappy jobs every day so they can afford paint. Or spending a few minutes with the guy who pushes his grocery cart down my street to talk about politics or poke through his scavenged goods for a treasure to barter for. Or watching the old Chinese ladies in my neighborhood do tai chi in the park in the morning. When you recognize and embrace the different ways you can give your life meaning and make a difference, from the smallest good deeds to tapping into your spirituality, you've found your religion.

Write
thank-you
notes for
everything.

If you're from the South or have a mother who lives by the words of Amy Vanderbilt or Emily Post, sending thank-yous for every gift and act of kindness is up there with brushing your teeth and changing your underwear every day. It's damn near vital to a civilized society. And it's not just a matter of good manners, although that's reason enough. Mailing a note to your grandmother to say "Thanks!" for a birthday gift or to the friend who picked up your mail while you were on vacation is common sense. And the older you get, the more you need to nurture the bonds with those people who consider you worthy of a trinket or favor. They're the ones who'll have your back when you're down and out, sick, or need a glowing recommendation. A simple gesture like a signed, sealed, and stamped letter—no quickie e-mails, please—makes you stand out from the plebes and sloths who don't. It's kind of like saying, "Thanks. I deserved it."

# Perfect your
# A.M. stretch.

**W**hether you're a gym fiend or a couch queen, spending a few minutes stretching in the morning is one of the nicest things you can do for your body and brain. And, let's face it: scraping yourself out of bed doesn't get easier as you age. Bending, pulling, and flexing wakes up your mind and your muscles in a natural, meditative way—even if you beeline to aerobics or the coffee pot right afterward.

Declare
your birthday
a national
holiday.

I t only comes around once a year and it marks one of the most significant days in your whole life, so it's your prerogative to make a big deal of yourself for the day. Notify your boss weeks in advance and take the day off from work so you can sleep late, watch game shows, and read trashy magazines over a champagne brunch, or do whatever it is you consider decadent and frivolous for the entire day. And since banks, dry cleaners, grocery stores, and all of those other mundane, errand-oriented businesses are generally closed on other holidays, consider them shuttered—and off limits—for your day, too. Your birthday is the perfect excuse for a day of pure, unadulterated loafing, goofing off, and behaving badly, so milk it while you can. Some people keep their birthday under wraps, as if admitting you're a year older puts another nail in the coffin, but reclaiming the day has nothing to do with your age. It's about you celebrating you. Not only do you score all of the perks, like free dessert or drinks and maybe a few presents from friends who might've otherwise forgotten, declaring a "me" day is the ultimate gift to yourself.

# Stock an emergency disaster kit.

As scary and depressing as it is to think of all the reasons you might need to crack into a stash of worst-case scenario supplies, it shouldn't stop you from getting a life-saving trunk together. In addition to storing a three-day supply of water (one gallon per person, per day) and nonperishable foods, like protein bars, granola, peanut butter, nuts, crackers, canned juices, and multi-vitamins, you should also have a Red Cross–approved first aid kit, a flashlight, and battery-powered radio with extra batteries, face masks, garbage bags, an emergency survival handbook, and a pen or pencil and paper. Whether the lights blink off for a few hours in a storm or you're faced with something more serious, having a fully-prepped emergency kit makes the same good common sense as the random assortment of "just in case" essentials we cram into purses every day. You'd never leave the house without a nail file, safety pins, breath mints, clear polish, powder, and other girlie survival basics, but this stockpile has a higher calling than stopping a run in your pantyhose.

Accept
compliments.

When someone says, "Sweet shoes!" or "You look fabulous!" or "You're a great artist!" something weird happens to a lot of women. We have this odd habit of deflecting any acknowledgment of our beauty, skills, or smarts. Compliments ricochet off of us, and we almost reflexively downplay our awesomeness with some negative comeback like, "Oh, these old things?" or "It's just the lighting." But this "aww, shucks" mentality is for the insecure. At your age, you've got more strength and self-assurance. You rock, and you know it, so why not admit it?

Minimize
pointless
drama.

The waiter forgot your side salad! A red sock slipped in and pinked your whites! You're stuck in traffic! Not one of these crises is worthy of an exclamation point, much less a nervous breakdown. We thrive on drama because it makes us feel important, but making mountains out of speed bumps is just bad policy. It takes too much energy to get hysterical over life's little wedgies, and all of the carping in the world isn't going to undo whatever inconvenience or hiccup has you in a twist. Besides, whipping yourself into a frenzy when you break a nail or The Guy doesn't call is tiresome to your audience. People lose interest in needless theatrics because it's boring to be around someone who always grabs for the spotlight. Drama creates anxiety, too. Hyperventilating over a bounced check or red wine stain only spikes those hormones in your body that breed stress. And who needs more stress? Learn how to spare yourself the agony—literally. Play it smooth when you get a speeding ticket or lose your keys for the nine billionth time. Shit happens to everyone all the time, but the people who sail through the small-time issues and barely register a complaint have an edge over the squawkers.

Unplug your
TV for a while.

**E**ven if you swear that the Discovery Channel and political documentaries make up the bulk of your TV-watching diet (yeah, right), turning off the boob tube for a week, a month, or a season will radically change the way you view your time and priorities. It's not enough to simply vow not to watch. Cancel your cable or yank the cord or roll your television into the closet for the duration, because if it's easy to access you won't be able to resist the temptation to tune in. While you're taking a break from the constant influx of depressing news, reality shows, bad reruns, and celebrity-obsessed dreck, you might realize what a crock the "not enough hours in the day" excuse is. Instead of plopping on the couch after a long day of work and getting a fix of TV zone-out time, you can do all of those things you swear you never have time for, like cooking dinner instead of nuking it, going for walks, or finally reading the stack of books and magazines accumulating next to your bed. Listen to music or NPR in the morning instead of the mindless background noise of perky news anchor banter. Play Scrabble instead of watching *Wheel of Fortune*. After a while, you'll notice how those hours that used to slip away so quickly—slurped into the glowing idiot box and regurgitated in the form of lame *Friends* reruns you didn't find funny the first time they aired—now just amble by, leaving you with plenty of time to hang out with your girlfriends, paint your toenails, and trawl eBay for shoe bargains.

Dye your hair
an outrageous
color.

It might be blond or purple or jet-black; the color itself is irrelevant. As long as it's crazy enough to warrant whiplash reactions from people who know you, consider it outrageous. Committing to a new shade is one of those low-grade risks that can kick-start your sense of adventure if you're in a rut. Or, when you're turning over a new leaf, say moving to a different city or beginning a new job, a shock of new hair is like starting with a clean slate. Sometimes it's those minor, superficial changes that have the biggest impact on how you feel and think. Because it takes a good bit of courage to dye your hair any color—much less one that'll stop your friends and family in their tracks—and it's exciting to open yourself up to the new attention when people compliment or comment. You start to see yourself as someone who can take radical change without worrying too much about the outcome or what others think. Adopting a new color says, "I don't take myself too seriously," and living that philosophy will serve you well.

Invest
in seriously
frivolous
undies.

The value of comfy cotton briefs is unquestionable, but every girl's got to have a panty drawer full of frilly, racy, barely-legal lingerie, too. Special occasions always call for a matching bra-and-panty set, and banishing panty lines with butt floss never fails to improve your rear view. Then there are those days when you need a mental lift, and simply feeling the silky, sexy texture and knowing you're wearing something naughty changes your whole attitude. Even if no one ever sees those lacy numbers, or the garter and corset getup just ends up in a heap on the floor, owning sexy undies is empowering, like Superman's knockout costume beneath his Clark Kent disguise. Underneath the plain-Jane, innocent outer layer that the whole world barely notices, there's a fiery, daring diva waiting to burst through the seams.

# Own your
# mistakes.

**Y**ou left a candle burning and torched your roommate's antique table. You forgot to feed your man's goldfish and it died. The crack about your brother-in-law's bad comb-over made the circuit, and he's not amused. It's a fact of life that everyone, everywhere the whole world over screws up on a regular basis. We ram our foot into our mouths, break things, and generally cause a lot of accidental chaos, but in a few simple words, we can make it all better. Our natural instinct is to deny or deflect any blame, like the leaders behind so many corporate and political scandals who proclaim their ignorance and innocence and insist they did nothing wrong. Rather than festering in guilt and coming up with a ream of excuses to try to explain away a mistake (which reeks of being unrepentant), confessing your sins is a shortcut to redemption. Few can hold a grudge against a genuine apology, and taking responsibility for your own foul-ups actually restores some of your dignity. It takes strong character and courage to admit you're wrong, and delivering an honest mea culpa means you've reached the pinnacle of maturity.

Take your
hobby more
seriously than
your job.

Unless you're unbelievably lucky or seriously in denial, what you do from nine to five every weekday is all about the paycheck; the daily grind is a means to an end and to health insurance. Jobs can be rewarding, fulfilling, and all of those other qualities that make you crawl out of bed every morning, but the interests you pursue (regardless of pay) are the ones that give you a strong sense of purpose and self. Maybe you're a world-class ice skater, or a culinary wizard, or a closet poet. We call these endeavors "hobbies," but even the title seems to trivialize their value. The creative outlets you plug in to are what makes you feel alive, and in the big scheme of things, that's way more important than a fat bank account or a good quarter for your company. But that doesn't mean you've got to quit your job to pursue a career in macramé or stargazing, either. It's a matter of getting your priorities straight and valuing your own satisfaction more than you fret about deadlines, employee reviews, and brownie points with your boss. Don't devote your life to a gig that doesn't reap equal returns; if you put in more than you get out of it, you're shortchanging yourself. Be passionate about the things that give your life meaning, and maybe, eventually, you'll find a way to make a living doing what you love.

Talk to
strangers.

It's a shame that one of the first things you learn once you're old enough to form complete sentences is that you shouldn't chat with people you don't know. It's a fine rule for kids, but unfortunately, the mistrust and uneasiness with chatting up strangers can carry on into your adult life. You don't quite know why, but it feels intrusive or awkward to break the silence. You pass some of the same "strangers" almost every day, and yet they're still anonymous, like the coffee shop barista you see every morning, the mailman, a waitress at your favorite restaurant—maybe even a neighbor you can't wave to without feeling weird. But striking up a casual chat with strangers is how you begin to feel connected to your adult identity. You get the sense that you belong to a neighborhood and a city if you can say "Hey, how's it going?" to a deli clerk and get a friendly response. Even if you only talk about the weather or traffic or some other inane topic, making human contact means you're not isolated and alone, that you're part of something bigger than your own little world of job, family, and friends. The more strangers you talk to, the fewer strangers there are.

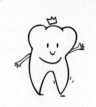

# Get health insurance.

I have a confession to make: I went several years without health insurance. (Sorry, Mom.) I probably could've afforded it, but writing that check every month would've strangled my teeny little social life. I was living in a new city, meeting great people, and I just wanted to hang out at bars and cafes and travel on the few extra dollars I had to spare. I went to clinics and paid out of pocket. I homeopathed aches, flus, and colds, and prayed my teeth wouldn't fall out. Finally, I broke down and signed up—a gift to myself for a birthday. It wasn't the perpetual fear of a broken bone that would set me back thousands to see a doctor that motivated me, or even the worry that I'd have to ask my parents to shell out the money to cover anything more drastic. (Sorry, Dad.) I just figured out that, for all the talk about being independent and smart, I still had yet to take full responsibility for myself. I won't lie—writing the check still grates on me. I still dream of canceling my policy and traveling somewhere exotic for three months instead. But around the time my check is due every month, when I'm going through the pissy turmoil of forking over my hard-earned cash, I comfort myself with the thought that, as much as it sucks sometimes, it's proof-positive that I can take care of me.

Hook up
something
high tech by
yourself.

*S*tart with the blinking clock on your coffee pot, or aim higher, like the ground-up installation of a new computer, or replacing your VCR with a DVD player. It's not as hopeless as you think. Once you plow through the instructions or, after figuring out which outies plug into which innies, the glowing sense of accomplishment you'll bask in is second only to the giddy feeling that you might just be competent enough to work for NASA. So what if you short-circuit the gizmo and cause a blackout in a section of your city's power grid? Even if you have to phone in some toll-free backup from customer service, technically, you're still doing the hook-up by yourself. You'll have that shining moment of clarity when you realize that lots of other electronic gadgets operate on the same plug-and-punch model. Never again will adapters, power strips, or hubs strike fear in your heart.

# Live through a blind date.

$\mathcal{G}$etting set up with a guy you've never laid eyes on is a rite of passage for every woman. Whether you snag him online or through a mutual friend, the whole process of preparing for the date and volleying from frenzy to fantasy on a minute-by-minute basis is the perfect blueprint for diving into any random, new experience. Maybe he'll be The One. Maybe he's an axe murderer. What if he's hot? What if he's a troll? Should I have an escape plan? Does he have one? Like starting a new job or signing up to run a marathon, the pangs of self-doubt and terror going into a blind date are balanced with awesome daydreams of being swept off your feet, romantic strolls in the park, and making beautiful babies together. Regardless of your worst fears or rose-tinted dreams, actually making it through the date, and realizing that it wasn't as awful or picture-perfect as you'd imagined, is the best reason of all to go for it. Every time you have one of those reality checks, you grow a bit more brave and less suspicious of the unknown. There will always be horror stories and fairy tales surrounding blind dates (or any scenario where your ego is on the line), but in the end, it always makes for one helluva story.

# Be a gracious guest.

You're approaching that age when being invited into a friend's or acquaintance's home involves more than dialing for pizza and showing up with a six-pack. Volumes of books have been written on the rules of proper etiquette for everything from social greetings to place settings, but being a good guest is the golden rule of social graces above all others. Anyone can learn the stickler manners, like using the correct fork or how to eat peas politely, but graciousness is more subtle and intuitive. You've been a guest enough times that you just *know* that it's never, ever okay to show up empty-handed, and that bringing a bottle of wine, a small plant, or a jar of outstanding honey is classier than high-fiving your hostess when you walk through the door. Unless you're fatally allergic, you realize that eating what's served, without mention of your weird aversion to lentils and other food quirks, is the thing to do. Some strange force beckons you to remove the sheets from your bed and refold hand towels when you spend the night in someone's home, even if your own place is a pigsty. I can remember my mom tidying up hotel rooms because she thought it rude and tacky to leave the place a mess for someone else to clean up. When you realize that being a guest is a privilege that comes with as many responsibilities as being the host, you've truly arrived at the grown-up table.

Escape
creeps and kick
criminal ass.

**I**f looks could kill, crushing the perves and freaks who try to hurt you would be easy. But they're persistent, nasty vermin, and you need more than a glaring, mean stare and a raised middle finger to scare them off. Even if you've got *Karate Kid* moves and a barrel of pepper spray tucked into your Gucci bag, you have to take a self-defense class to truly be prepared for an attack. It's easy to get blinded by your own tough-girl act and think that you're quick and gutsy enough to beat an attacker. But when you're caught off guard, bravado liquefies into sheer panic, and your badass self can barely move, much less put up a defense. As much fun as it is to learn those eye-gouging, groin-kicking techniques, these classes teach you more than just how to fight back. They give you confidence and deprogram the bogus mind-set we're wired with that says kicking, punching, and screaming are unladylike. A determined psycho might out-muscle you, but arming yourself with steely nerves and the chutzpah to survive gives you a better shot at out-smarting him.

Invest in earplugs.

**D**on't buy a couple; get a whole bottle of those foamy, orange bullets and plant pairs in every purse and coat pocket in your closet. Earplugs can whisk you to your own muted Eden when you're surrounded by urban racket and distracting sounds that are so loud you can't hear yourself think. They're a pillowy buffer between you and pounding jackhammers, screaming ambulances, chatty airplane seatmates, and the guy facing into a trough of popcorn behind you in a movie. Maybe it's a sign of age and crankiness that these things can ruin your day or wreck your concentration, but when you're on edge, blocking out the constant stream of sound that bombards you can make your worldview more Zen. Watching a weary mom soothe her wailing baby or taking in an overcrowded subway platform is poetic and sweet when your ears are cushioned. And there's also that small matter of protecting your hearing. You might feel like an old fart, sticking them in your ears when you're at a rockin' concert or over-cranked action movie, but you'll be thankful when you're thirty-five and can have a conversation without screeching, "EH? Wha-?" like your grandma.

Lose
your virginity.
Again.

Let's be honest: the first time around for most of us was awful or awkward or forgettable, and most likely all of the above. Chances are, you barely knew what you were doing; it was hardly the sacred, meaningful encounter it was cracked up to be, and you just wanted to get it over with. But when the time is right, you should reclaim your virgin status and hold out for the guy who proves he's worthy of it. You don't have to renounce your previous sexual encounters or strictly abstain until you're married. When you do meet a likely candidate, set a slower sexual pace and take your time exploring each other before you go between the sheets. Don't give in to every lusty urge, but satisfy your curiosity about who he is and what you want instead. Then make your second first time the sweet, satisfying romp you only wish you could have had way back when. Do the roses and candlelight, or the roaring fire and champagne, or whatever romantic, sentimental scenario the two of you cook up to make your first time together more hot and fun and meaningful. Getting into each other's pants is the easy part. When you wait a little longer and make sex about the *moment* rather than just clearing a hurdle, you set the stage for a deeper, more honest relationship because you actually have to *talk* about sex before you do it. What you get is sex that isn't just about desire, but sex that is passionate. Anyone can want, but passion requires wisdom, commitment, and respect.

# Know your blood type.

Like you need a reason? Here are a few: 1) so you can donate blood when your type is in short supply; 2) if you're attacked by vampires and need an emergency transfusion; 3) it's the perfect conversation-starter at a dull dinner party; 4) in case of a real emergency, you could save someone else's life.

Confront someone who's done you wrong.

An ex-boyfriend who lied or cheated? A friend who spread your secrets? A hairdresser who butchered your hair color? However big or small the slight, if you've been burned and it still stings, you owe it to yourself to face off and get some closure. A lot of times, we suck up our anger and hurt because talking about it only dredges up the old pain, or we think we're pathetic for not being able to move on. But you can't really get on with your life if an old wound is echoing in your head. You'll feel like a spineless weenie for getting burned *twice*—once for the wrong, and again for letting the culprit get away with it. Work up the courage and have your say. Even if you don't get an apology (or a new dye job), speaking your mind is cathartic. Instead of lugging around the dead weight of being wronged, you're handing it back to its rightful owner.

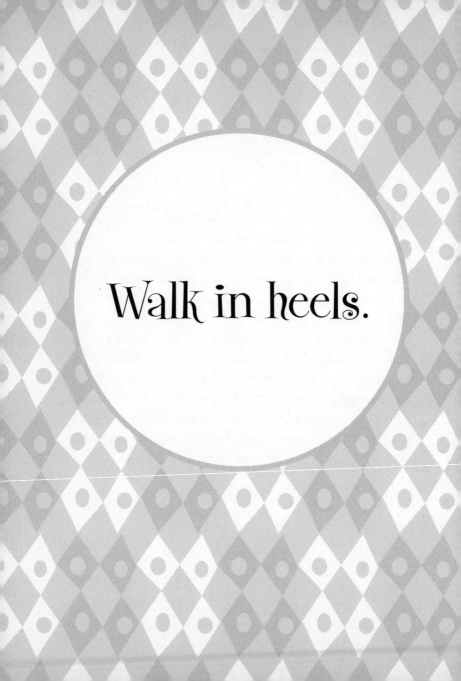
Walk in heels.

$\mathcal{S}$**trutting** in stilettos without looking like a teetering clod is a difficult skill, but one worth mastering if you want to waltz into rooms and feel more classy than klutzy. Like it or not, flats, sandals, and sneakers will never be suitable shoes when you're wearing a flashy dress or floor-length ball gown. Some women were born to wear strappy, spiky heels, but for the rest of us, it takes more practice. The trick is to break in your feet slowly and test your high-heeled dogs in the privacy of your home before you make a wobbly debut in public. The pinching, throbbing sensation eventually goes numb, but the pain is a fair trade-off for those Cinderella hours when you look elegant and graceful and stand a few inches taller. Plus, perfecting your heel-toe shimmy gives you major advantages when you want to see and be seen in a crowded room. Best of all, if you're prone to slouching, the tiptoe stance gives you bombshell posture, arching your back and hiking your butt and boobs to high alert. No matter how cozy your tennis shoes are, they can't do that.

Write a body manifesto.

**D**raft a declaration of independence from harping on your body, because it's too easy a target when things aren't going well. A bad day at the office, a fight with a boyfriend, or even a trip to the mall that turns sour because nothing fits right—for some reason, we can shift our anger or disappointment with a random, unrelated bummer onto a so-called flaw we see in the mirror. We think, "My stomach pooches out too much" or "I'm too flat-chested." It's important to have a written reminder of your body-positive principles, like "I won't blame my thighs when my jeans are tight; I'll curse the designer." In your journal or on a sticky note hung next to your mirror, write a policy that covers head to toe all of the ways that you can be nice to your body. What form of exercise feels so good it doesn't seem like work? When are you the least self-conscious of how you look? What do you love about your body? Tune in to what your body wants and needs, not what your brain is telling you. Whether it's losing a little weight, committing to a regular workout, or upping your energy level, get it on record so you can't keep ignoring it. Let your manifesto be a fresh start—a way to wipe out the past and move forward.

Watch the
sun rise and set
on the same day
by yourself.

When you need some quiet inspiration or to restore some balance in your off-kilter schedule, wake up when it's still dark out and watch the pink-orange layers of daylight simmer higher and higher above the horizon, until the sun is out full yolk. End your day the same way, following that big, descending ball of fire until it disappears from view. Who really knows why witnessing daybreak and dusk is such a spiritual, romantic event? Maybe it's because even when you're totally alone, you still feel irrevocably connected to and awed by something so big and powerful in action. We barely register the sun's movement throughout the day, but taking the time out to watch it during those crucial moments seems to slow time and make the present more real. Maybe it's not so much that sunrise and sunset are so magnificent, but that the very act of consciously stealing those bits of time to be still, silent, and completely in the moment is so rare.

# Disagree.
# Out loud.

**I**t's your inalienable right to be contrary. Open your mouth and say, "I don't think so." Practice speaking it out loud over and over until it rolls off your tongue as easily as saying "My name is . . ." Then take your new favorite phrase public. Don't stand on the outskirts of meaty conversations nodding and agreeing like a compliant sheep if the voice in your head is screaming, "Nuh-*uh!*" Step up and state your case about a political scandal. Engage in debates about what's in the news and argue your point, even if it's about what some starlet wore to the Oscars. Get used to the idea that your opinions and judgments are as valuable and important as anyone else's, and that being cowed into silence because it's not a popular opinion is an insult to what you believe in. Too often, we follow the pack and swallow our voices because it's infinitely easier on the ego. That empty, "Uh-oh, they're not gonna like me" feeling in the pit of your stomach keeps you quiet, but claiming your opinions does wonders for your conviction. It challenges you to defend what you believe and makes your opinions more concrete. Your heart beats a little faster, your face is flush with confidence, and you feel more alive when you register dissent, which beats being flatline and boring any day.

# Memorize your ring size.

**D**rop in on a good jeweler and have your ring finger measured. It's like your bra or shoe size—a girl's got to know such vital bits of information about herself. We think rings are for the engaged or betrothed, but waiting for a man to come along and buy you The Rock is almost as sad as putting together a hopeful-bride scrapbook of your dream wedding. Rings symbolize commitment, fidelity, and infinity, which isn't exclusive to romance. Knowing your fit means you can go shopping for pretty, sparkly things regardless of your relationship status. You're entitled to be good to yourself, for any reason, and if a couple of carats will remind you to be faithful and true to yourself forever, go for it.

Have a mantra.

Come up with a catchphrase that gets you through those fleeting moments when you want to chicken out, quit, or stay in bed for seven weeks. When the nagging voices in your head start messing with you, saying things like "You'll fall on your face" or "Better safe than sorry," you need to be able to megaphone yourself an internal message that'll shout down your self-doubts and fortify your determination. For a while, my mantra was "I'm not going to end up in a cardboard box." It's not exactly easy to chant, but when I quit one job and decided to move across the country with no job, home, or trust fund waiting on the other end, it really helped to crystallize the faith I had in myself. In my mind, it meant that even if it was the worst decision I'd ever made, I still had the wits to take care of myself. Any time I freaked out about not having a forwarding address, those words helped me focus on the absurdity of the situation instead of the terror, and made the risk feel more like an adventure, not a tightrope walk over a fire pit. That's what good mantras do: they steel you against your uncertainty and catch you before you fall between the cracks.

# Research your family's medical history.

I know that talking about Aunt Myra's bunions or Grandpa Joe's wicked dandruff isn't exactly dinner conversation. And it's sort of depressing to find out who died of what in your lineage. But it's important to get some details on the health of your family tree, particularly your parents and grandparents. Although you're not necessarily destined for their exact medical fates, you need to know if there's a genetic predisposition for major diseases and mental health issues in order to keep an eye out for symptoms, get checked regularly, or start preventative treatment. If it's as serious as breast cancer or as mortifying as raging halitosis, the best part is that you've got a built-in support group to talk to about how to spot, treat, or avoid whatever ills run in the family.

Do it somewhere risky.

$L$ike sneaking out after curfew or falling in love with a rebel when you're a teenager, having sex in an unorthodox place is a rite of passage into adulthood. It's not about the thrill of getting caught or the heightened excitement, because in all honesty, it's always a bit more awkward and unsexy than you imagine. There's the gearshift jabbing into your butt, the sand or pine needles chafing your skin, or the sight of stuffed animals and trophies in your old bedroom that make it uncomfortable or a little weird. The real kick comes later, when you're settled down and not "allowed" to be as wild and careless as you can be right now. The memory of doing the deed somewhere crazy only gets better with time, and rather than sulking about how stable and normal your life has gotten, it's your permanent confirmation that you lived it up like there was no tomorrow when you had the chance.

# Open a bottle of champagne.

**I**t's time to air kiss your lowbrow glory days goodbye. They were good, no, *great* while they lasted, and the fact that the only fizzy drink you consumed came out of a keg, well, that was a blast, too. But things are changing. You're getting a taste for the good life. You're graduating from paper and plastic to china and linen. You own clothes that are dry clean only, and you actually obey them. But the one skill that symbolizes your newfound sophistication like nothing else is the ability to crack open a bottle of bubbly without spraying it everywhere. Whether you spend a fortune on the real stuff occasionally or save your dime on sparkling wine for all occasions, popping it open takes poise. Here's the trick: don't twist the cork. After you remove the foil and the wire restraint, wrap a towel around the neck and cork, hold the cork, and slowly spin and pull the bottle away.

# Make more money than you spend.

$J$**ust** thinking about 401(k)s, IRAs, or bond funds can put you to sleep or, if it's around April fifteenth, make you feel anxious and irresponsible. Everyone agrees that saving money is a drag. A hot rock massage and an avocado facial today is so much more appealing than a down payment on a house in five years, even if owning a home is your ultimate, lifelong dream. That's why building your little nest egg is one of those hallmarks of adulthood you have to embrace early, before you're strapped with a mortgage or kid expenses. You can't ask your parents for money when they're drawing Social Security, and you can't screen out angry creditors with Caller ID forever. Getting your financial status in the black isn't a downer if you think of it in terms of making more than you spend—a more positive spin on the saving philosophy. Instead of the scrimp, skimp, and deny vibe that saving has, the new philosophy says "work toward a promotion" and "ask for a raise." Having some cushion in your bank account isn't just about weathering unforeseen expenses or saving for a big purchase. It's a sign that you're earning your worth instead of spending your potential.

Be a nudist
for a day.

**F**or a second (or ten or twelve hours), forget your body issues. Strip off your pjs and be totally, utterly, nekkid-as-the-day-you-were-born bare-ass for an entire day—in the privacy of your own home or secluded wilderness, of course. We spend so much time fussing about the layers that go on top, it's easy to forget the beauty of what's underneath it all. And it's a super-sensory experience. You start noticing things like how your muscles flex when you pick up a glass, the feel of everyday textures like hard wood or soft carpet against your bare skin, and the way your tummy or thighs bounce and jiggle when they're completely free—things that you normally take for granted or find fault in. If you can let yourself be unabashedly naked, you're giving yourself permission to love your body. Just be careful of sharp edges.

# Adopt
# an awkward
# teenager.

**G**rowing old isn't exactly fun, but it's easy to forget that growing up can be even more brutal. You've probably blocked out the worst of your puberty years—including those fuzzy perms, bitchy girl mobs, and mortifying changes to your body—but there's a girl out there who's living and dreading it right now. Take her out for coffee and compliment her outfit. Ask her what she's reading or teach her how to drive stick. Tell her your most humiliating date story and show her your freshman yearbook picture. In short, give her a break from the confusing, hormone-riddled havoc that she wakes up to every day. Befriending her may be therapeutic for you, a chance to confront and exorcise some of those old demons from your high school days. It'll keep you clued in to everything that's now, hip, and young, and might even show you ways to deal with your own grown-up dramas. But hanging out with her is a selfless deed that can spare her some of the same agony you endured because you're showing her she's not alone. Being the fabulous and cool mentor-sister-friend isn't a résumé-builder, but the payoff is priceless.

Eat soy.

I**f** sneaking a little tofu or soy milk into your diet sounds about as appealing as eating Styrofoam and dirt, you're setting yourself up for a health crisis. Getting at least twenty-five grams of soy per day carries a long list of potential health benefits, including lowering your risk for heart disease and cancer, easing the symptoms of menopause, and preventing osteoporosis and diabetes. You lived on diet soda and cheese toast throughout your teenage years? Your body was in a constant state of change and growth back then, so there was no real harm done. But now that you know better, your body is actually less forgiving than it was back then, and who could blame it? You know all of the reasons it's good for you, but think about it this way: starting a new soy habit might make you feel less guilty about those occasional french fry and milkshake binges.

# Dress for longevity.

**B**efore a big date or a night out with friends, most of us spend hours primping and fluffing in the bathroom and plowing through the closet for a snazzy, sexy ensemble. There's nothing wrong with wanting to look dynamite, but we forget one cardinal rule for having a great night: Be comfortable. We skip out the door looking perfectly put together, but just a few short hours later, the whole look hits its past-due point. The pantyhose are sagging at the ankles, the control-top underwear are riding high and digging into flesh, the blisters are chafing, the hair has wilted into a heap of tangled hay, and any minute the push-up bra could completely cut off the blood flow to your head. Even if you manage to suck up your misery, all that squirming and suffering is painfully obvious to the people you're with, and the party's over—according to your outfit—even if the night is still young. But you don't have to wear sweatpants or leave your hair in a permanent ponytail to extend your nightlife. Spend the extra dough on better shoes and line them with strips of soft moleskin where they might rub. Ask your hairdresser to show you how to style your mop so it doesn't expire too early. Fine-tune your all-nighter wardrobe so you always have a layer to take off or cover up with, like a great wrap. When all is said and done, the nights you remember for the rest of your life aren't defined by what you wear or how you look, but how effortlessly they played out. Getting decked out to live it up until the night is officially over all but guarantees a great one.

# Kick one habit.

**G**reat intentions are a load of crap. Some of us struggle an entire lifetime to finally stop some irritating or nasty habit, but until you make peace with your weakness or finally put an end to it, that annoying practice will camp out in your psyche and be a constant reminder of all the ways that you suck. Every time you light up a smoke or catch yourself gnawing your cuticles to ribbons, there's a neuron firing in the deep recesses of your brain telling you you're weak and worthless. Pinpoint the addiction that's got you in a headlock, whether it's your obsession with checking e-mail or a more serious yen that threatens your health, and commit yourself to quitting. Breaking a habit is hard work, but doing it solo is even harder—and severely cuts your chances for success. Find a support group, therapist, or friend who can help you through the rough days when your willpower dips, and pat you on the back when you have a breakthrough. When you finally beat a bad habit, you've got the master key to your self-control. If you ever want to deal with other baggage or sort through old issues, you've got a mental guide to acknowledging, accepting, and recovering from whatever ails or irks you.

Defy gravity.

The gravitational pull that keeps the Earth in orbit is an awesome, amazing thing. Unless, of course, you have breasts. Then, the scientific wonder isn't so much about the invisible forces that keep you grounded, but how they contribute to the unmistakable downward drag of your once-perky assets. The migration is slow but inevitable, and there's only one surgery-free way to fight the natural process: a righteous bra. You might think, at this point, that you know your girls best and that they're properly propped, but you're probably wrong. You stuff 'em into frilly, sexy, water-padded demi-cups, but chances are, the last time you gave support any real thought, your mom was in the dressing room tugging at your ta-tas and telling the ancient salesclerk you needed a smaller size. All the more reason for having a professional fitting while your boobies are still gorgeous. Whether you go to a department store or fancy lingerie boutique, these nice ladies have seen every shape, size, and droop imaginable, and will tell you if a bra is squeezing your back fat or pulling your boobs apart or any of the countless other ways that a bad bra can let you—and your girls—down.

# Own a cashmere sweater.

Yes, it's nothing more than overpriced goat hair, but no closet is complete without this soft, rich fiber because it holds the power to make a girl feel so good. More PC than a mink (since it's shaved, not skinned) and more decadent than angora, wear cashmere and no matter how crabby or low-rent you look, this fur will make you feel like a million bucks. There aren't many textures that can add an aristocratic edge to a simple pair of jeans, but cashmere has a cachet that is up there with diamond earrings and martinis. With a little scrimping and saving or devoted bargain hunting, you can add cashmere to your stash of other quintessentially grown-up girl accessories (think pearl earrings, high heels). Like a fake ID but the real deal, cashmere says "I can pass for an adult," even if you still feel like an imposter.

Use a great
dermo.

**M**oles shaped like dinosaurs . . . wrinkles . . . sun spots that rival Gorbachev's birth mark . . . miscellaneous skin damage from rolling in baby oil and laying out on aluminum foil before SPF was invented. It happens. Or, it will. That's why you've got to scout out the best skin doctor in town—and don't settle for the hack your cheap-ass HMO recommends. You can't stop the ravages of time from tap-dancing on your face, but you *can* slow it down before your skin is the texture of a Louis Vuitton bag. Vain? Perhaps. But you're only looking after what Mother Nature gave you. And if a monthly facial or microdermabrasion is what it takes, so be it.

# Get over yourself.

From the summer after fifth grade when I hit my growth spurt—all arms, legs, and no boobs or discernible curves—I had a major complex about my height. Too plain to model, too spastic for sports, I evolved into a bookish wallflower and did everything in my power to avoid attracting attention. I think people mistook my self-consciousness for icy aloofness, but I just assumed that the boys I had a crush on were afraid of me. I developed a skill for self-deprecation, pointing out all of my flaws and quirks to anyone within earshot, and carried this goofy MO all the way through college. I pursued only what came easily to me, from the school I chose to the guys I dated to the courses I signed up for. One night during my senior year, killing time with a roommate, I was rattling off the list of reasons I'd bumble any run-ins with the scruffy, arty boy I was in love with ("I'm too tall and spazzy," "The hole in the armpit of my sweater will show"), when my roommate broke in with the best bit of advice a girl could ever ask for. "Jesus, girl. Get over yourself," she blurted. "Do you really think you're so noteworthy that people notice everything you do or say? People are too busy having their own weird internal monologues to really care anyway." Harsh as they were, her words were like a Get Out of Jail Free pass. Years of neurotically trying to protect my fragile ego from other people's judgments trickled away when it finally occurred to me that most people have more on their mind than me. We all need an occasional reminder that the world doesn't revolve around our paranoid fantasies, and those three words will never fail you when you're deep into the abyss.

# Sleep in a hammock.

**S**noozing and swinging make the entire world vanish. Wrapped in the loose hug of a hammock, the back-and-forth rocking lulls you into a lazy stupor. The fact that you're not doing laundry, baking cookies for the homeless, or paying bills seems completely beside the point. Hammocks are all about free afternoons with nothing but a good book, an ice-packed glass of something sweet, and the slow breeze that nudges your swing while you sleep. There's no pressure or schedule, and the only reason you bother to leave the "to-do" free-zone is to refill your glass. It's about letting yourself be utterly lazy—and loving it.

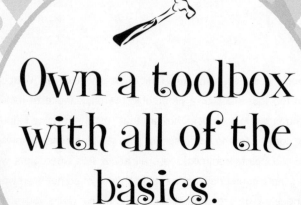

Own a toolbox
with all of the
basics.

**D**on't wait for the handyman of your dreams to waltz into your life and fix all of your wobbly doorknobs and build you bookshelves. Boldly go where too few women have gone before: the hardware store. Find the sweet old guy with a tape measure clipped to his suspenders (every store has one), and tell him you want a sturdy toolbox with real gear—not the stenciled girlie one with petite pink-handled tools and thumbtacks. Even if you only bust it out when you need to hang a picture, having the right tools for any job means you don't have to pull the damsel in distress act every time something leaks, breaks, or needs tightening. At the very least, you need a full-size hammer, an adjustable wrench, pliers, at least three different sizes of flat- and Philips-head screwdrivers; small, medium, and large nails, a level, a tape measure, and, if you're feeling really bold, a staple gun. Just try not to look so excited and eager when Mr. Suspenders asks you if you need a stud finder.

# Jettison your "skinny" jeans.

They're sitting in the way back of your closet, crammed next to your old prom dress and an ex-flame's sweatshirt, waiting for the day when you stop eating chips and join a gym. They've got such great sentimental value because they're from the good old days, when the only exercise you got was from beer runs or dancing on tables, and wearing them practically guaranteed a great night out. Now, you're just hanging on to jeans that are two sizes too small, praying for that miraculous moment when you can zip them and still breathe—as if fitting into your old party pants will mark the defining moment when your eternal youth and ideal weight are frozen in time. Until then, they're a constant reminder of how big your ass is, how lazy you've gotten, and how long it's been since you boogied till sunrise. If you're clinging to clothing from back then, frame it, scrapbook it, or set it on fire, but keep it where it belongs—in your past. A pair of jeans can't bring back your twenty-one-year-old buns or those wild nights, no matter how long you hold on to them. If the day comes when you can slip into your old size, buy yourself a brand-new pair to break in with new memories.

# Collect correspondence with friends.

I f you keep in touch via e-mail, save all of the back and forth rambles with your closest friends. At my first job in Los Angeles, I printed out every exchange I carried on with one of my soul sisters who was in medical school in New Orleans at the time. Two years later, when I moved on to another gig, I sent the ream of old e-mails to her bundled in a binder. Back in the day, people saved every shred of mail because it was so rare. The old e-mails I saved weren't exactly profound literary genius, but collectively, they made up a two-way digital diary of our lives during an intense time for both of us. It was crammed with sage twenty-one-year-old advice, the bizarre and hysterical realities of our new lives, and all of those fears we had that, at any moment, our "adult" cover would be blown. Unlike a private journal, which carries only *your* take on life, a string of letters between friends holds a three-dimensional slice of time. It's the perfect gift to pay homage to the friendship or, if you're not so sentimental and she has a sense of humor, a book of blackmail to be excerpted at her wedding reception.

# Get a massage.

Having at least one professional rubdown in your twenties isn't a luxury—it's a must. Book the massage, write it in your calendar, and presto, it's a legitimately scheduled appointment like any other date, only it's not about a client or a visit to the doctor, but something purely for your pleasure. When you show up ahead of time, you get to lounge in a thick bathrobe, take a steam or hot shower until your brain is jelly and slowly, as you sip lemony water, the angst and mental "to-do" lists you carried into the spa seem harder to hang on to. Stepping into the dimly lit room, where your serene massage therapist tells you to get naked and slip between the sheets, feels like getting a warm, friendly hug—almost like rolling back into the womb, with its cozy, ambient vibe and quietly pulsing New Age music. Then the massage starts, and any anxiety you had about letting a stranger stroke your body vanishes, and you pray time is passing even slower than it seems so the feeling lasts longer. The natural ritual of doing the spa experience, along with the massage itself, makes the practice feel like a sacred form of self-worship. By the end of the appointment, the initial guilt you had over doing something so self-indulgent is replaced by one thought: What's so bad about being good to yourself?

Memorize your favorite smells. Surround yourself with them.

$\mathcal{S}$**pend** some time in a natural foods store or perfumery to sniff and sample the vials of essential oils. Search for the scents you love and the ones that remind you of vacation, naps, and food you'd like to bathe in. Invest in those smells. Drip drops into your bathwater, under the floor mats in your car, and on cotton balls that you flick under your bed and into your desk drawers. Anyplace where you're likely to spend a few hours, plant your scent. Every now and then, you've got to take a power-break from your life, even if it's just a minute-long hiatus to block out the bad tuna sandwich you had for lunch. Women have a more fine-tuned sense of smell, and if you can train your brain to cooperate, you only have to close your eyes and inhale to make a dumpy job or mountain of paper-work fade into the background. It won't make you skinnier, prettier, or smarter, but it might keep you from pitching a stapler through a window or setting a pile of dirty laundry on fire.

Fall in love
(or lust)
without
blowing off
your friends.

Instead of going MIA and dropping out of your social circle every time you find a guy you're mad about, stay in the loop. Arrange weekly get-togethers, circulate catch-up e-mails, or insist on a night out every now and then. When you get so wrapped up in him that you're out of touch with your friends, you run the risk of becoming utterly boring, like the girl who lives for her job. Even the best jobs (or men) get old if that's all you have going on. Besides, your friends are the ones who will snicker in all the right places when you talk about the kinky stuff you're doing with him, or bring you double-stuffed chocolate or cheesy foods if he turns out to be a jackass.

Dub the
"Greatest Hits"
from your
childhood.

Compile a soundtrack that captures the highlights of your family life before you were old enough to judge music, and make copies for every member of your family. Think about the camp songs you belted out until your parents threatened to tape your mouth shut, and the road-trip tunes you listened to over and over. There are the musicals you still know all the words to, and the melodies your parents unconsciously hummed while they cooked dinner or drove you to school. All of those songs are burned into your memory like certain smells and tastes, and as terrible as the music may seem now, it's an instant reconnection with that time in your life when cooties and vegetables were your biggest worries. The music is an inside joke that only your people will get, and it's a supreme compliment to them, too. If you can pick through your wonder years and find those golden hits, it's because you've got great memories to mine from.

Care about
where your
food
comes from.

If you've ever read the ingredient label on a box of cookies and gotten the heebie-jeebies, or spent a little too long pondering the seventy-eight varieties of cereal in a grocery store aisle, it's probably because it's dawning on you that what you put into your body affects more than the size of your butt. But unless you live on a farm or grow your own veggies, you're completely cut off from the food chain. You buy nuclear, processed food wrapped in slick packages and sanitized produce that pushes the limits of Mother Nature's intentions, like those picture-perfect tomatoes that show up in the middle of winter and taste like soggy cardboard. Most of us are totally disconnected from what we eat because we're too busy to think about the farmer who produced it or the impact it has on the environment—much less how to pronounce some of those ingredients. What the hell is xantham gum, anyway? But small steps, like buying more organic stuff, shopping at farmer's markets, or joining a farm co-op can bring you a little closer to the source. It's not a crime to eat a Ding Dong or bio-engineered asparagus, but making more conscious choices about the food you consume is a wee bit better for the planet—and your love handles.

# Fly first class.

Whether you scam a free upgrade, cash in your frequent flyer miles for the perk, or splurge on a vacation ticket, you've got to know the luxury of what goes on behind those curtains. The hot hand towels and bottomless cocktails are just the beginning. Aside from that certain wicked satisfaction you get from watching coach passengers trudge past and covet your leg room and pre-takeoff snack, flying first class gives you a taste for the life you so deserve. Instead of playing elbow hockey for an armrest or choking down a sample-size bag of pretzels, you can kick back and daydream about ways to get a piece of the pampered life. Maybe you can't afford it on a regular basis, but at least you'll know it's not so out of reach or unfathomable to be catered to like a premier client.

Cultivate your own style.

Copping looks straight out of magazines and experimenting with trends isn't a fashion faux pas when you're still trying to get a grip on your identity. Are you the foxy, skintight-mini type, or more hippie-dippy flowing skirt chick? Do sleek, tailored suits fit your life, or do laidback, casual chic clothes? Playing around with your style and wearing whatever mode you're in at the moment is part of the fun of being indecisive, unpredictable, and twenty-one. But as you approach thirty, you get a better feel for what fits and what makes you feel like you're in someone else's skin—and seriously uncomfortable. Why fuss with iffy fads or styles that look incredible on doughnut-deprived models? Toss the green Mary Janes you *so* want to be cool enough to pull off, the serious interview suit you'd never really wear to an interview, and the preppy college sweaters that are waiting for a comeback in your closet. It's not that you have to choose a uniform and eschew everything that's funky or unusual for you, but you should weed out the wish clothes and hone your instincts for the colors, shapes, and styles that look fabulous on you. Buy two of anything basic, versatile, and comfy, splurge on an occasional piece that's drop-dead stunning, and build your wardrobe around what you love-love-*love* to wear. You'll still spend hours plowing through your closet trying to decide what to put on, but at least you're narrowing your options.

Carry something to read, a notebook, and a pen at all times.

You never know when artistic genius will strike, or when you might get stuck in an obnoxiously long line, and having these three essentials can spare you the mental ass-kicking you'll give yourself for not having anything to do or write on or with when you need it most. Instead of lapsing into a comatose stupor during your train commute or going postal on the housecoat-clad lady in line ahead of you at the grocery who's waving around forty-three expired coupons, you can immerse yourself in the soothing prose of a novel or jot down a list of the things you'd rather be doing instead of buying toilet paper.

# Forgive your parents.

We all have baggage that's been handed down to us from our parents and their parents and so on. But there comes a point in your adult life—and the sooner the better—when you have to stop blaming them for every issue and hang-up you have that you can trace back to childhood damage. As cliché as it sounds, they did the best they could. And even if they were certifiably awful, lugging around bitterness is only going to hurt you even more in the long run. If family pain is seriously affecting your life, find a great therapist who can guide you through recovery and, if not forgiveness, acceptance of the hand you were dealt. Or find your own ways to make peace if you've got run-of-the-mill grudges against them. Parents are easy targets, but holding them responsible for sour relationships and every other failure you've suffered stifles your growth and keeps you from seeing your own shortcomings. Besides, seriously bitching about your parents when you're pushing thirty screams "early mid-life crisis." Deal with your mental health issues now, before they're etched in too deep.

Be a dork.

For years, we do our best to hide our alter ego, that spazzy, un-cool chick who really wants to stay home on Friday night and watch nature documentaries or play Scrabble. Now that you're in a place where, truly, you could give a flip about what other people think, it's time to set her free. You can dance and flail by yourself in a crowded club, and it won't ruin your social life. You can stand up for the coworker who gets picked on or talked about when she's not around, and not care if the "cool girls" will still like you. You can wear rainbow-colored socks, and your friends will think you're funky. You can admit you love ABBA and The Carpenters, and col-lect stamps, and faithfully watch *Little House on the Prairie* reruns. You can crochet a crooked, nine-foot purple scarf and proudly claim it as your own handiwork. Whip open your journal and scrib-ble a list of all of those instincts you squashed and interests you kept in the closet because you didn't think they were chic or clever enough. Now's your only chance to make up for lost time.

# Stop slamming other women.

*G*irls can be so bitchy sometimes. We're all guilty of saying nasty things about each other, like calling the fox in a tight mini a skank, or gossiping about the skinny blonde who got a quick promotion. It's probably part of some ancient biological instinct that we need to stomp all over the "competition," but it's a good time to evolve beyond the cave-girl rivalry. We need to stick together instead of sniping about each other. With all of the other inequalities and hardships we face—like the fact that we *still* make less money than men at the same jobs and have to put up with piggy comments from old-school boors—the one thing we should be able to count on is the camaraderie of our sisters. We're all in the same boat, so own up to your insecurities instead of taking them out on other women. Save your spite for the beer-bellied construction worker who waggles his tongue at you or the client who pats you on the ass and calls you "sweet thing."

Get waxed
down there.

**D**on't blush or cringe or get your feminist panties in a twist. It's just a plot of hair—not a political statement—and it's yours to do with what you will. Even if you only do it once, do it because it's damn funny, not because you think it'll improve your sex life or make you feel better about yourself. It won't. Do it because you've always been curious, but too chicken, and you won't have to shave (if you do) so wearing a bathing suit is slightly less nerve-racking. Do it so you know, once and for all, whether it's worth the few minutes of scorching pain and humiliation to have a perfectly manicured lawn.

# Adopt another motherland.

The country you were born in is like family: familiar, easy, comforting. But as you get older, you need to branch out to get a taste of life outside your own little bubble, like going off to college. Finding a second homeland means traveling and exploring the world beyond your borders until you find a place that embraces and nurtures you like your first "family" does. It's where you let your guard down and know the names of streets and the owner of your favorite restaurant. Being considered a local here is the biggest compliment. You can always escape to this country without stressing about the exchange rate or finding the right place to stay, because you already know those things like you know your own phone number. You speak the language and love the people and know the land. This country stands out from all of the other far-off, thrilling places you've visited because it's not a destination that's only rosy when you're on vacation. You know you could dig in and make a life there, too. There's probably something deep and profound about adopting a new country, like how it makes you worldly and smart and interesting. Then again, it's also selfish and lazy, but in a good way. Like family, this country will always be there for you and expects nothing back. Half the reason you love it is that you don't have to try very hard. You can never have too many places to call home.

Tell someone
your deepest,
darkest secret.

**W**hatever it is that weighs heavily on your conscience, it's never as bad as you think it is. But secrets are the boogie monsters that lurked under your childhood bed when the lights went out. In the dark, they're terrifying. You expect them to leap out and scare the bejesus out of you any second, so you keep your head buried under the covers, imagining the worst. Eventually, you get tired of being afraid and grow bold. The lights go out and instead of cowering, you whip off your covers and shine a flashlight under there—and there's nothing but dust bunnies. Rather than letting your secret fester and grow in your head, saying it out loud takes the bite out of it. Then something funny happens: you create a new, stronger kinship with the friend you confessed to, and she divulges her own deep, dark secret. It's called the reciprocity effect, and it's why women have an edge over men when it comes to health and happiness. We have an easier time revealing our feelings and fears, so our girlie chat sessions aren't frivolous—they're free therapy.

# Make a killer cocktail.

**R**egardless of how much or how often you drink, knowing the recipes for classic cocktails, like martinis or gin and tonics, and learning how to pour them flawlessly are important steps in every girl's life. When you have dinner parties—and you *should*—whipping up a batch of your favorite cocktail makes up for other skills in the entertaining department that you might lack, like cooking or flower arranging. Your guests will never notice the mismatched flatware or the charred meatloaf if they've had an immaculate drink.

# Read your
# old diaries.

**Y**ou'll cringe. You'll laugh out loud. You'll be completely shocked. Flipping through your life in the pages of a journal is excruciating and humbling and hilarious. It's more than a trip down memory lane; it's an experiment in self-discovery. The truth as you lived it in ink, from the breathless catastrophes that consumed your whole world to the boring daily minutiae, provides a window into who you were and how far you've come. Will you learn anything deep and meaningful? Does it make you a better person? Can it solve your current problems? Probably not. The beauty of an old diary is that it's frozen in time. What you glean from its pages says everything about who you are now and what you've learned in the meantime. And buried somewhere in the drama and drudgery is enough confirmation that you've come a long way, baby.

# Tie a few knots.

We put so much weight in tying *the* knot, but hardly know a figure eight from a Granny knot. One thing's for sure: relationships are much harder to figure out. Go online or get an eager Boy Scout to teach you the ropes, and memorize a few key knots, including the classic Windsor tie. This is one of those survival skills that come in handy when people least expect you to be useful, like securing a boat to a dock or strapping big things to the roof of a car. Tying knots is such a *guy* thing, and half the reason it's such a satisfying rush is hearing your inner badass holler, "*DAMN, I'm good.*" The other reason? Maybe the fact that you can tie pretty knots on packages. Or maybe it's good to know that you can lash someone to a chair with confidence. It's your call, really. What you do with it is your business.

# Have your fortune told.

Whether or not you believe in palm readings, tea leaves, or Tarot cards, it's always fascinating to hear someone else's take on your life and where it might be headed. Before you hit the big 3-0, you've got to revel in the fact that, if nothing else, you have years and years of potential ahead of you. Will you find love and have kids? Is there a better career out there waiting for you? Will you ever pay off your student loans or get out of debt? If you ever question why you're here and what's really important to you, you only have to consider the things you'd ask a fortune-teller to reveal. The issues you're most curious about point to the destiny that you want—you just have to own up to the fact that you have more insight and say in your fate than you think.

Cry often.

**T**ake a cue from Holly Hunter's character in the movie *Broadcast News*. Every now and then, turn off the TV, close the door, unplug the phone, and bawl your eyes out. For the dreadful day at work, the really happy ending, the depressing news segment, or whatever moment that makes your nose run and eyes well up, sob until your tear ducts run dry. Most of the time we try to stop ourselves from all-out, full-body boo-hooing like it's a sign of weakness, but shedding tears is the body's way of releasing stress hormones. It's the best relief and release from the low-down blues, and it shows that you're not afraid or ashamed of your emotions, even if you do wind up sniffling over a broken shoelace or a few extra pounds. Chances are, you have a pile of other reasons to justify a good breakdown, and letting it all out means you're owning your issues and purging them properly, instead of taking it out on your boyfriend or the delivery guy.

# Give yourself
# flowers.

**U**nless you're fooling around with a florist, chances are, you don't get flowers nearly as often as you deserve. Make a habit of buying yourself a bouquet of your favorites. Gerbera daisies or roses, poppies or tulips, having something fresh, alive, and colorful around is good for your soul. Invest in a few different size vases, break up a bunch of flowers, and dot a few rooms with them. We spend so much time indoors—in cubicles staring at glowing boxes, at stores, in gyms, and commuting to and from work—that we're hardly ever in touch with living, breathing nature. Something as simple as a vase of flowers on your desk or near your bed can keep you closer to your roots. It's a mistake to think of flowers as a birthday, anniversary, or special occasion treat, because you don't need a reason to be good to yourself. For all the good they do, they should cost double.

Stop looking
for a soul mate.

The fairy-tale romance is a nice thing to think about when you're fifteen, but now that you've been through a few relationships, it's time to stop looking for Prince Charming or expecting your guy to conform to impossibly high standards. Whether you're currently attached or on the market, reign in your expectations for the perfect love. Real love is hard enough work, but constantly searching for the guy who's going to fulfill all of your needs, or trying to turn your man into The Perfect Mate, is futile. The idea that there's one guy out there who fits you in every way and will complete you, is the myth that makes potentially great relationships a disappointment. You think that The One won't forget your birthday, or he'll write poetry about you, or all of your friends will adore him, so you're inevitably let down and think there might be another guy out there waiting for you whenever he fails those tests you've created to see if he meets your tough standards. Or you overlook great guys who don't fit your ideal criteria. But the truth is, the kind of lasting, phenomenal love that you're looking for doesn't just happen when you hook up with the right person. You have to be willing to grow and change and compromise to have a healthy relationship, but you can't do those things if you're only on the hunt for a soul mate. He might love stock car racing instead of great authors, forget to notice a new haircut, and think beer is a major food group, but if he respects you, is willing to talk things through and makes you feel great most of the time, hang on and see what happens. Think about it this way: you're probably not the independently wealthy, football-loving beauty queen some men would define as the perfect woman, but the good ones won't hold it against you, either.

# Give props
# to a teacher.

# Give yourself a make-under.

If a name or face doesn't pop into your head immediately, think back to one of your turning-point moments—when you realized you were great at *something*—and give credit to the person who helped you get there. It might seems sappy or cliché to send a thank-you note to a high school teacher or college professor years after the fact, but the sad truth is, they rarely get the thanks they deserve. Acknowledging their influence on your life is a step toward embracing your own brilliance, too. You have to have a certain amount of pride in where you are and what you've accomplished to thank someone for helping you along. Plus, it's good for your karma. You didn't get this far in life alone, and putting those grateful vibes out there might open another door for you to meet someone else who will rock your world.

# Learn how not to be a flake.

**W**e're all guilty of saying "yes-yes-yes" to too many invitations and pleas for help, but when you always punk out at the last minute because you're tired or something better comes up or you really don't feel like helping an acquaintance move into her five-floor walkup, you get a reputation for being unreliable and finicky. If you accept an offer to meet for drinks or you volunteer to lend a hand, don't give yourself an easy out anytime you have a lame excuse to flake. Either force yourself to follow through on your w̶ or don't agree to it in the first place. Instead of reflexively a̶ ing "Sure!" to every plan or job, train yourself to say, "̶ back to you?" or "Maybe." You spare yourself a worl̶ second-guessing when your word is good.

**E**liminate a time-consuming primping move or extraneous products from your beauty routine. Do you really need a forty-five-minute shower, three styling products in your hair, half an hour to blow dry, or a layer of heavy foundation and two different powders? Go to a professional—a hair stylist or makeup counter clerk you have history with—and ask her to help you streamline your regimen. Trimming even fifteen minutes from your daily ritual means you've got a little more time to read the paper, stretch to wake up or, let's be honest, sleep. There's this hideous myth that the older you get, the harder you have to work to look good. If anything, it should take less and less time because you're more comfortable in your own skin and your time is more valuable. So put your mirror time into perspective and lighten up. You have more important things to do than curl your eyelashes.

# Be notorious
for something.

It's nice to be known for your wholesome qualities, like making the perfect lasagna or crocheting doilies, but being infamous is a whole lot more fun. Maybe you slithered and writhed on a dance floor after too many shots of tequila and caused a ruckus between a guy and his date. Or maybe you pitched an antique vase into a brick wall in a fit of fury. Mooned a school bus full of nuns? Mailed a cow patty to your ex? Made out with a bartender in an alley? Whatever the bad-girl deed, it's got to be the kind of thing your friends won't let you live down. Having a masterpiece moment, when you cut loose and let your wild, dangerous side out regardless of the consequences is one of those girlie privileges you can't pass up. We're stereotyped as hysterical, moody, impetuous, irrational creatures, so you might as well take advantage of it occasionally. Half the fun is getting into trouble, but the rest is in reliving the wicked, mischievous act every time your girlfriends start telling "Remember when . . . ?" stories.

Bounce back.

When you've been mercilessly dumped or you've put a tragic relationship out of its misery and your heart is feeling like a deflated balloon, it's part of the process—and certainly justifiable—to crawl into bed with a bucket of ice cream and not come up for air until the aching, throbbing pit in your stomach goes away. We've all been there. But having wallowed in low-down heartache a few times, I figured out that there's something more important than going through "the process"—i.e., shock, shame, power-eating, denial, and anger. My heart had been stomped on, and I was tucked into a fetal ball listening to Aretha Franklin sing her broken soul songs when it hit me. Every woman has a little bit of the Queen of Soul in her—that tough and tender natural woman who has suffered worthless men; dark, hollow disappointment; and given everything only to have someone take even more. But it's not the experience that makes you stronger. It's our ability to embrace heartache, find strength in our weaknesses, and wear our scars with pride—to make poetry of our pain—that helps us bounce back. Because in the end, your worst moments are really a testament to your strength and courage.